I.   Introduction

Economic theory suggests that a firm with some lines-of-business subject to rate-of-return regulation and other, non-regulated lines-of-business may find it profitable to alter the actions of its regulated businesses in order to increase the profits of its unregulated businesses; in effect, circumventing the regulation. The literature on regulatory evasion has discussed two means by which such a firm might act to circumvent regulation. First, under cost-plus regulation, the regulated firm may have the incentive to cross-subsidize (also known as cost-shift), whereby the firm subsidizes the unregulated business by shifting a portion of the costs incurred by the unregulated business into the ostensive operating costs of the regulated business (see e.g., Posner (1969), Brennan (1987), Noll and Owen (1989)). Second, when an unregulated business is in a vertical relationship with an affiliated regulated business, the regulated entity may have an incentive to refuse to deal with rivals of the affiliate, or only deal with the rivals on worse terms than it would have had it not been regulated (see e.g., Brennan (1987), Beard, Kaserman and Mayo (1996), Economides (1997), but see also Sibley and Weisman (1997)). To counter this incentive, regulators may require that the regulated firm deal with all users of its input on equal terms. If regulation is less than perfect, then subtle forms of discrimination may persist, such as reducing the quality of the input provided to the non-affiliated firms.

To the extent that the on-going regulatory oversight necessary to prevent such discrimination is costly or imperfect, these theories provide an economically-coherent basis for prohibiting regulated firms from owning vertically-related businesses.[1] While this provides a theoretical justification for the prohibition, one cannot infer that the prohibition is welfare-enhancing. Even if the discrimination hypothesis is empirically valid, there may be efficiencies associated with a regulated firm's entering an vertically-related market that are sufficient to offset the welfare loss from the discrimination. These efficiencies may be reflected in lower prices, or higher quality. Hence, the case for the prohibition depends not only on the existence of a non-trivial loss from the discrimination, but also on the premise that the efficiency gain from integration is small.

This paper contributes to our understanding of the empirical relevance of the discrimination

---

[1]The literature on vertical integration to evade regulation is distinct from motivations discussed in the general literature on vertical integration (for a review of the latter see Perry (1989)). The rationale for integration in the regulated context is most closely related to an older literature on tying as a means of regulatory evasion (see, e.g., Bowman, (1957)). In that literature, the regulated firm ties the regulated product to some unregulated product, and charges a price for the bundle greater than the sum of the tying good's regulated price plus the tied good's market price. Indeed, one can view discrimination as a form of tying, whereby the regulated entity makes purchases of the input (or more generally, makes the quality of the input) conditional on buying the output from its affiliate.

hypothesis and of efficiencies from integration in two ways. First, we develop a framework for formalizing the notion of discrimination, and show that discrimination increases the profitability of the unregulated affiliate of a regulated firm. We use this framework to generate implications of the discrimination hypothesis, and also of the hypothesis that integration lowers the cost of improving quality. Second, we empirically examine an industry in which conditions for discrimination exist. In providing cellular phone service to consumers, cellular phone companies use an input supplied by the local phone company (or *exchange carrier*[2]) to produce its product (a phone call between a customer served by the cellular company and one served by the local exchange carrier). That is, connection to, and use of, the local exchange carrier's (LEC) facilities is necessary to the production of a call between subscribers of the two networks. The price that the LEC can charge for the use of its facilities is regulated. In addition, there are exaclty two cellular phone providers in each market, and the local exchange carrier is permitted to own equity in one of the two. In fact, the dominant local land-line carrier almost always holds a majority equity interest in one of the two cellular carriers. Thus, under the discrimination hypothesis, there is an incentive for the regulated firm to offer different terms to its affiliate and the affiliate's rival.

A feature of this industry that makes it useful for evaluating the discrimination hypothesis is that the extent of vertical integration between the LEC and its affiliated cellular company varies across geographic markets. In particular, there is considerable cross-sectional variation in the share of the cellular company's equity owned by the dominant LEC and also in the share of the relevant physical assets (land lines, switches, etc.) owned by the dominant LEC.[3] These differences can be thought of as differences in the extent of vertical integration across geographic areas. We show that one prediction of the discrimination hypothesis is that as the LEC's equity interest in its cellular affiliate falls, its incentive to discriminate decreases. Similarly, as the ownership of the relevant physical assets becomes more diffuse, the ability to discriminate falls. Increased discrimination leads to higher prices, while the efficiency hypothesis implies that (holding quality constant) increased concentration of ownership of the cellular company, and of the relevant physical assets, should reduce price. Because of the variation in both types of ownership concentration, we are able to test whether higher concentration is associated with higher prices and lower average quality as predicted by the discrimination hypothesis. Moreover, to the

---

[2]The common industry parlance for a local telephone company is a local exchange company (LEC) because they operated the various community-level telephone exchanges.

[3]That is, in some geographic areas, there are multiple, non-competing land-line carriers. For example, the same two cellular companies cover the entire Los Angeles metropolitan area. However, the monopolist LEC is different in different parts of the area; both Pacific Telesis and GTE served significant numbers of land-line customers in the area during the period we examined.

extent that both discrimination and efficiency occurs from integration between cellular companies and land-line monopolists, policy-makers would be interested in the net effect on cellular phone prices and quality. Our analysis indicates whether on net the two effects increase or decrease prices and quality, and hence addresses a central policy question.

We find that, consistent with the discrimination hypothesis, prices increase with the share of the cellular company's equity held by the dominant land-line provider. Similarly, prices increase with the share of the relevant physical facilities controlled by the dominant LEC. While this evidence is consistent with the discrimination hypothesis, it could also be consistent with integration leading to efficiencies if quality increases were associated with integration, and if those increases more than offset the effect of higher prices (at least to the marginal consumer). To test whether the higher prices reflect higher quality, we examine the relationship between several (subjective) indices of customer "satisfaction" and the ownership measures. The evidence implies that, controlling for other factors, satisfaction is increasing in one measure of the degree of land-line ownership (the percentage of lines served by the dominant LEC) and decreasing in the other (the dominant LEC's share of interconnection facilities). The effect of financial ownership on satisfaction is small. This seems to suggest that both discrimination and efficiencies result from greater integration. The quantity regressions yield similar implications; quantity increases with the dominant LEC's share of lines served. This suggests that, despite higher prices associated with integration, consumers' perception of quality is increased by greater integration. At the same time, quantity falls as the dominant LEC's share of interconnection facilities rises, suggesting that some of the price increase is due to discrimination.

The issue of whether to allow regulated firms to enter related, unregulated businesses has emerged in several regulated industries. Probably the most prominent example involves the regional Bell operating companies. Under the 1982 Modified Final Judgement in the AT&T antitrust case, these providers of local phone service have been prohibited from entering long-distance phone service.[4] One of the reasons for the prohibition was a concern that these firms would discriminate against rival long distance carriers (see Brennan (1987)). These companies recently petitioned the FCC to vacate this order.[5] The regional Bell operating companies presented a significant amount of evidence in support of their position. For

---

[4]U.S. v. AT&T 552 F. Supp 131 (1982). The 1996 Telecommunications Act provides for eventual Bell operating company integration into long distance services. Currently, they are allowed to compete in long-distance carriage between local markets they do not serve. The discussion in the text relates to long- distance carriage in which one party to the call resides in the local market in which the regional operating company is the local monopolist.

[5]See "Motion of Bell Atlantic Corporation, BellSouth Corporation, NYNEX Corporation, and Southwestern Bell Corporation to Vacate the Decree," Civil Action No. 82-0192 (July 6, 1994).

example, they hired 47, mainly economic, experts, including three Nobel laureates, to present evidence they thought would be helpful to their position. Likewise, the long distance carriers, led by AT&T, MCI, and Sprint, hired many respected economists and other experts to argue against RBOC entry into long distance.[6]

Most of the empirical evidence presented by these two groups dealt with the issue of the size of the gain from introducing additional competitors into the long-distance market. Little evidence was presented concerning the potential for regulatory evasion through cost-shifting or discrimination (see, however, McChesney (1995)). In general, these issues have proven difficult to analyze empirically in the context of long-distance telephone service because of a lack of a suitable natural experiment. Some anecdotal evidence that the concern over discrimination is valid in this and other industries has been offered, yet there appears to be no systematic empirical investigation of the issue. Because the relationship between cellular phone companies and LECs is analytically quite similar to the relationship between long-distance phone companies and LECs, we think that our analysis provides some evidence relevant to that industry. We find evidence that LECs have discriminated, but also that there are efficiency effects of integration. In the cellular industry, the effects appear to be roughly offsetting. It does not follow, of course, that the magnitudes relevant to the trade-off between losses from discrimination and gains to integration will necessarily be similar in other telecommunications markets, or in other regulated industries. However, our results do suggest that the potential for both discrimination and efficiencies are real.

II.   Background

Cellular phone services use FM radio transmissions to provide mobile communications. Accordingly, the FCC allocated a portion of the radio spectrum to be used for the provision of cellular telephone transmission. Under FCC regulations,[7] two licenses, called the 'A' and 'B' licenses, were awarded in each metropolitan area to firms to build cellular transmission systems and provide cellular service at the wholesale level.[8] The FCC's decision to issue two licenses, and thus allow two firms per

---

[6]See for example, "AT&T's Opposition to the Four RBOCs' Motion to Vacate the Decree," (Dec. 7, 1994), Civil Action No. 82-0192.

[7]*In the Matter of an Inquiry Into the Use of the Band 825-845 MHZ and 870-890 MHZ for Cellular Communications Systems; and Amendments of Parts 2 and 22 of the Commission's Rules Relative to Cellular Communications Systems*, Report and Order, CC Dkt. No. 79-318, 86 FCC 2d 469 (1981).

[8]During the sample period, only cellular phone companies offered mobile phone service. Recently, firms using an alternative radio transmission technology, PCS, have begun providing a similar

market, represented a compromise between the benefits of issuing relatively few licenses, and allowing firms to realize potential economies of scale within the limited spectrum available, and the benefits of competition from issuing a large number of licenses.[9]

One of the two licenses in each market (typically, the B license) was reserved for a local provider of land-line phone service. The FCC required the cellular licensee to be run separately from the land-line company (ies) that own it. In some markets there was a single such landline provider, and it was awarded the license. In other markets, there were multiple (non-competing) providers, and the FCC's choice of licensee among these candidates was to be made through "comparative hearings."[10] However, the FCC encouraged the LECs in each geographic area to reach a settlement, whereby all but one of the candidates withdrew from consideration. Such a settlement was reached in all of the 30 largest markets (which were the first markets for which licenses were awarded). In other markets, settlements were also common. Typically, the company receiving the license was jointly owned by all of the relevant local LECs.[11] Award of the other, "non wireline" licenses was also initially determined by comparative hearings, and settlement among the candidates often occurred here as well.

Each cellular service area is divided into a honeycomb of geographic areas, referred to as "cells." Within each cell, there is a "cell site" where radio signals are transmitted to and received from mobile units. Because these broadcasts are made at low power, the same channel of spectrum can be used simultaneously in nearby (but not adjacent) cells without interference. The signals received by each cell are transmitted to the Mobile Telephone Switching Office, via a land-line or microwave link. For most calls, the signal is then linked through a tandem switch to the land-line network. In this way, interconnection to LECs is a necessary input for completion of most cellular calls (over 90% of cell calls are completed on wireline networks). Local exchange carriers are usually regulated in regard to the pricing of this input. In particular, there is a maximum price that the LEC can charge for interconnection, and also a requirement that the LEC deal with the two cellular services on a nondiscriminatory basis.

An issue we address in some detail is whether the quality of cellular service differs between

---

service.

[9]For a detailed discussion of the technological and regulatory history of cellular telephony, see Calhoun (1988).

[10]Our discussion of the history of FCC licensing derives primarily from Rosston (1994).

[11]Given the potential for side-payments between the parties, it would seem that ownership of the new company would be determined so as to maximize the joint profits of the LECs. As discussed in Section III, profit-maximization would dictate that the distribution of the cellular firm's equity would reflect the distribution of physical assets within the geographic area.

cellular companies in each market, and across markets. The source of these difference is not primarily differences in broadcasting technology; the analog technology used to transmit cellular calls duringour data period was the same for all cellular systems in our sample. Rather, cellular service quality differs primarily in call blockage rates (due to system congestion) and call interference (due to gaps in system coverage).

Two common problems that reduce the quality of cellular service are "dead spots" and "hot spots" within cells. Dead spots are areas within cells in which cellular transmissions can experience noise and interference leading to the transmission being "dropped." One can be talking on a cellular car phone while driving through a city and suddenly hear substantial static or interference and lose the transmission. This problem can be a result of such things as local topography or physical obstructions such as tall buildings.[12] Hot spots are small, localized areas of a city from which an unusually large number of cellular calls originate. Hot spots typically develop at freeway exits and entrances or busy intersections. Radio engineers designing cellular systems have often had difficulty predicting where hot spots will appear. Roadway construction or repair can sometimes permanently remove or create "hot spots," and random events such as traffic accidents can suddenly create temporary ones. Hot spots can strain a cell's capacity, blocking the transmission of calls or causing calls to be dropped during the "hand-off" as a car moves into a cell that is experiencing an unexpected "hot spot." The common solution to "dead spots" and "hot spots" is splitting these cells in order to create more channels. In general, the greater the number of cells per system subscriber, the less frequent will be these types of problems, and the better will be the overall quality of the cellular system.

Since competing cellular providers may make different decisions regarding the number and location of cells in a market, differences in transmission quality may arise. Moreover, the nature of hot spots and dead spots is such that the optimal location and number of cells in a particular system change over time. Adding cells to the system can require coordination between the LEC and the cellular company, since a new cell requires trunk lines connecting it with the land-line network. The coordination problems may give rise to differences between affiliated and independent cellular companies. In particular, if integration mitigated these coordination problems, one would anticipate differences between how affiliated and unaffiliated cellular companies route their calls to the LEC network. For example, industry sources tell us that unaffiliated cellular companies tend to build their own link between their cell sites and their Mobile Telephone Switching Office, whereas affiliated cellular companies tend to lease a high capacity line from the LEC. As discussed in Section III these differences may be evidence of a more

---

[12]Calhoun (1988, p. 96) discusses an actual case in which the appearance of leaves on trees in the spring created a "dead spot" along Philadelphia's Schuykill Expressway.

6

efficient production procedure or of discrimination.

III. A Model of Quality Differences

As noted above, the existence of an unregulated affiliate may cause a regulated firm to change its actions so as to increase the profits of its unregulated business. In particular, if regulation is less than perfect, then subtle forms of discrimination may persist, such as reducing the quality of the interchange services provided to non-affiliated firms.[13] Alternatively, quality differences between the affiliate and its rivals could be due to efficiencies from integration. For example, integration may reduce the transaction cost of contracting for the construction of new trunk lines to connect a new tower. These lower transaction costs allow the affiliate to be more responsive to changes in demand for cellular services.

To formally evaluate these two potential sources of differentiation between affiliates and non-affiliates, and to derive empirical implications of each, we model the difference between the firms as a difference in unambiguously defined "quality." This type of "vertical differentiation" seems a natural way to capture potential differences between telephone service providers. In particular, it provides an intuitive way of thinking about the effects of LEC ownership of cellular companies on quality. Given this characterization of potential differences between firms, we consider a two-stage game. In the first stage, each LEC determines the quality of interconnection it will provide each cellular company. In the second stage, the two cellular companies simultaneously choose prices, given the interconnection quality from stage 1.[14] We solve for the equilibrium using backward induction. That is, we first solve for the equilibrium cellular prices as functions of the firms' qualities. This allows us to calculate comparative static derivatives to demonstrate how prices and output vary with quality, and to discuss the implications for profits. Given these relationships between quality and cellular company profits, we then consider LEC's decisions regarding quality determination. In particular, we formally analyze how the incentive to discriminate varies with observable characteristics of ownership structure. Using the comparative static

---

[13]Here, we use the term "interchange services" to refer to any service provided by the LEC to the cellular phone companies that can alter the quality of cellular service. Hence interchange services include the speed of a cellular customer obtaining a dial tone, the sound quality of a call between a wireline and cellular customer, or the delay and negotiation cost faced by the cellular company in obtaining new trunk lines to connect a new cell to its system.

[14]The model described here essentially assumes that the LEC's decision regarding interconnection quality completely determines cellular quality. In a more general model, we could allow an intermediate stage, in which the two cellular companies simultaneously choose the quality of their products, given the quality of interconnection services from stage 1. The cellular companies would then choose prices in the third stage, given these qualities. This generalization would better reflect the cellular companies' decisions as characterized in section II, but would not change the basic results of our model.

relationships, we then derive implications for the relationships between LEC ownership structure and prices, output, and quality. Finally, we contrast these to the empirical predictions of the hypothesis that vertical integration leads to efficiencies.

The model is based on the framework developed by Shaked and Sutton (1982). The basic idea is that consumers choose one of several available versions of a good, and consumers all have the same ordinal ranking of those products (ignoring price differences). Hence, if all versions of the product had the same price, then all consumers would choose to buy the same product, which they would all view as being the highest quality product.[15] To reflect the market structure of interest, we characterize cellular markets as having two competing products. Let the quality of the two products be Z_B and Z_A where $Z_B > Z_A$ We generalize the Shaked and Sutton (S&S) model in two alternative ways. First, unlike S&S, we allow some consumers to drop out of the cellular market as prices rise. Let consumer i's valuation of product j be $x_i Z_j + \theta_i$, where x_i can be interpreted as consumer i's marginal value of quality. Consumer i will drop out of the market if $x_i Z_j + \theta_i < P_j$, for all j, where P_j is firm j's price. Conditional on making a purchase, consumer i buys product B rather than product A iff $x_i(Z_B - Z_A) \geq P_B - P_A$. In this way, consumers segment themselves on the basis of their x_i, with higher valuation consumers buying the higher quality product. One can think of this model as examining changes at the extensive margin; how the number of cellular customers changes with quality. This generalization comports with one of our empirical measure of sales; the percentage of customers subscribing to cellular phone service. The alternative generalization examines the intensive margin; i..e, it holds the number of customers fixed, but allows each to vary her intensity of use. This approach is presented in Appendix B.

A. Downstream Equilibrium

To see how ownership by LECs affects the equilibrium, consider first the rivalry in the cellular, or "downstream" market. In keeping with the FCC's license labeling, let firm B be the cellular company affiliated with LECs, and let firm A be its only rival. Each has constant marginal cost of $C = W + R$, where W is the LEC interconnection charge, and R are the other costs. Let Z_B be the quality of the affiliate cellular company's service, and $Z_A < Z_B$ be the quality offered by its rival. A positive level of sales for firm j implies $Z_j + \theta > P_j$. As noted, for any given set of prices, those consumers who place the higher value on quality will buy from firm B. At the most general level, Firm B's demand is

---

[15]This contrasts with a model of "horizontal differentiation", in which consumers differ in their ordinal ranking of products, so that even if the goods had the same price, all consumers would not choose to buy the same product.

$$q_B = \int_{\frac{P_B-P_A}{Z_B-Z_A}}^{X} \int_{P_B-xZ_B}^{\overline{\theta}} q(x,P_B)g(\theta,x)\,d\theta\,dx \tag{1}$$

where $g(\theta, x)$ is the joint distribution of θ and x, where x varies from 0 to X, and θ varies from 0 to $\overline{}$. To derive implications from this model, we follow S&S in assuming that $\theta_i = \theta$ for all i, and that x is uniformly distributed with support $(0,1)$ (so that $F(x) = x$ for all $x \in (0,1)$).[16] S&S assume that demand is completely inelastic in that all consumers purchase the product. We generalize this somewhat by allowing each consumer to have a "choke" point; consumer i buys nothing if $x_iZ_j + \theta < P_j$ for all j, and buys one unit if this inequality is reversed for some j.[17] That is, changes in P_B and P_A affect quantity demanded by changing not only the market shares of the two firms, but also the number of consumers purchasing the good. This assumption provides the foundation for the "extensive margin" version of the model. In Appendix B, we consider the "intensive margin" version, in which the number of consumers purchasing the good is fixed, but where $q(x,P_B)$ is allowed to vary continuously.

Given these assumptions, B's demand is

$$q_B = \int_{\frac{P_B-P_A}{Z_B-Z_A}}^{1} f(x)\,dx = 1 - \frac{P_B-P_A}{Z_B-Z_A}.$$

B's objective function is

$$\Pi_B = \left(1 - \frac{P_B-P_A}{Z_B-Z_A}\right)(P_B - C), \tag{2}$$

and its best-response function is

---

[16] S&S also assume a uniform distribution, and our characterization of the distribution of consumers is equivalent to theirs when $\theta_i = \theta$ for all i. We relax this assumption in Appendix A.

[17]In fact, we assume that the cost of providing cellular service, $C \geq \theta$, so that not all customers are served in equilibrium.

9

$$P_B(P_A) = \frac{P_A + Z_B - Z_A + C}{2} \tag{3}$$

Similarly, A's objective function is

$$\Pi_A = \left(\int_{\frac{P_A - \theta}{Z_A}}^{\frac{P_B - P_A}{Z_B - Z_A}} f(x)d(x) \right)(P_A - C) = \left(\frac{P_B - P_A}{Z_B - Z_A} - \frac{P_A - \theta}{Z_A} \right)(P_A - C) \tag{4}$$

and its best-response function is

$$P_A(P_B) = \frac{(P_B - \theta)Z_A}{2Z_B} + \frac{C + \theta}{2} \tag{5}$$

Solving equations (3) and (5) simultaneously, we find

$$P_A^* = \frac{Z_A(Z_B - Z_A) + Z_A C + 2Z_B C + 2\theta(Z_B - Z_A)}{4Z_B - Z_A}$$

$$P_B^* = \frac{(Z_B - Z_A)(2Z_B + \theta) + 3Z_B C}{4Z_B - Z_A}$$

$P_B^* > P_A^*$ as long as $Z_B > Z_A$. The issue of primary interest here is how efficiencies and discrimination affect prices. In terms of the model, efficiencies are parameterized as increases in Z_B, while discrimination is parameterized as reductions in Z_A.[18]

Proposition 1: Consider a market with two firms, and let the quality of those firms' products be Z_A and Z_B, where $Z_B > Z_A$. Denoting firm i's (i= A,B) price as P_i, we have

a. $\partial P_B^*/\partial Z_B > \partial P_A^*/\partial Z_B \geq 0$. Also, $\partial P_A^*/\partial Z_B = 0$ implies $P_A^* = C$ for all Z_A, Z_B.

b. $\partial P_B^*/\partial Z_A < 0$, and $\partial(P_B^* - P_A^*)/\partial Z_A > 0$

c. $\partial P_A^*/\partial Z_A$ is non-monotonic, and $\partial^2 P_A^*/\partial Z_A^2 < 0$. In particular, if $(Z_B - Z_A)$ is small, $\partial P_A^*/\partial Z_A < 0$.

<u>Proof:</u> a. $\partial P_B^*/\partial Z_B = (8Z_B^2 + 2Z_A^2 - 4Z_B Z_A + 3Z_A\theta - 3Z_A C)/(4Z_B - Z_A)^2$, which is positive since $Z_B > C - \theta$ and $Z_B \geq Z_A$. $\partial P_A^*/\partial Z_B = 3Z_A(Z_A - 2C + 2\theta)/(4Z_B - Z_A)^2$. This takes the sign of $Z_A - 2C +$

[18]As noted above, we do not formally model the determination of Z_A and Z_B by the downstream firms. Rather, we assume that they are completely determined by the actions of the LEC(s). In a more general model, the actions of the LECs change the cellular companies' cost of increasing quality, and consequently change equilibrium values of Z_A and Z_B.

2θ. To sign this expression, note that in order that A's price exceeds his cost, it must be true that

$$P_A^* = \frac{Z_A(Z_B - Z_A) + Z_A C + 2Z_B C + 2\theta(Z_B - Z_A)}{4Z_B - Z_A} \geq C \leftrightarrow Z_A \geq 2C - 2\theta$$

That is, in equilibrium $Z_A \geq 2C - 2\theta$. This implies that there are two characterizations of P_A; either $Z_A = 2C - 2\theta$, in which case $P_A = C$ for all values of Z_B, or $Z_A > 2C - 2\theta$, so that P_A is monotonically increasing in Z_B. If $Z_A - 2C - 2\theta$, then it immediately follows that P_B^* increases faster with changes in Z_A than does P_A^*. If $Z_B > 2C - 2\theta$, then the difference can be written

$$\frac{8Z_B^2 - Z_A^2 - 4Z_A Z_B + 3Z_A(C - \theta)}{(4Z_B - Z_A)^2} > \frac{3Z_A(Z_B - \theta + C)}{(4Z_B - Z_A)^2} > 0.$$

b&c. $\partial P_B^*/\partial Z_A = 3Z_B(-2Z_B + c - \theta)/(4Z_B - Z_A)^2$, which is negative since $Z_B > C$.

$$\frac{\partial P_A^*}{\partial Z_A} = \frac{Z_A^2 + 4Z_B^2 - 8Z_A Z_B + 6Z_B(C - \theta)}{(4Z_B - Z_A)^2}$$

From part a., we know that $Z_B \geq Z_A \geq 2C - 2\theta$, where the second inequality is strict except when $P_A^* = C$ for all values of Z_A. If there is strict inequality, then for $Z_B - Z_A$ sufficiently small, this expression is negative. As Z_A falls, the derivative rises, and eventually become positive. Evaluating the difference between the derivatives, we find that $(P_B^* - P_A^*)$ increases as Z_A falls. ∎

Proposition 1 shows that P_B^* increases as the difference between the quality of the two products rises, while the effects on P_A^* are less clear cut. One way of understanding these results is that increases in Z_B and reductions in Z_A serve to both increase B's quality advantage and increase the differentiation between the two products. Both effects increase P_B^*. The two effects work in opposite directions on P_A^*. Evaluating $\partial P_A^*/\partial Z_A$, one can see that at $Z_B = Z_A$ the derivative is negative, and more generally, the increased differentiation effect dominates when Z_B and Z_A are similar, while the first effect eventually dominates, as Z_A falls. For example, for $C = \theta$, the derivative is positive for $.54 Z_B < Z_A$.

Proposition 2 Greater discrimination leads to a reduction in aggregate sales.
Proof: Using the envelope theorem, the change in quantity induced by a change in Z_A is

$$\frac{\partial q}{\partial Z_A} = \frac{\partial q_A}{\partial Z_A} + \frac{\partial q_B}{\partial Z_A} = -\frac{(P_B - P_A)}{(Z_B - Z_A)^2} + \left[\frac{P_A - \theta}{Z_A^2} + \frac{P_B - P_A}{(Z_B - Z_A)^2} \right] = \frac{P_A - \theta}{Z_A^2} > 0.$$

Hence, a reduction in Z_A reduces the number of customers buying the product. ∎

Although discrimination reduces aggregate sales, it increases q_B. Hence, increased discrimination allows the affiliate to increase both its price and its number of subscribers, and hence its profits. While increasing discrimination reduces the number of customers, in this version of the model, efficiencies do not increase the number of customers buying the good. The reason is that in equilibrium, any consumer who prefers to not buy the good (i.e., consumers with x_i sufficiently low that $x_i Z_j + \theta < P_j$ for all j), necessarily prefers product A to product B (i.e., $x_i Z_A - P_A > x_i Z_B - P_B$). In that case, increases in Z_B induce some of A's customers to switch to B, but does not induce any non-customers to buy the good. In the more general model presented in the Appendix A, however, we show that increases in Z_B will induce some customers to begin buying from B. In either case, increasing Z_B increases the affiliate's profits.

To summarize, increases in the affiliate's quality increases both prices, and in the more general model, aggregate subscribership. Decreases in the rival's quality increase the affiliate's price and reduce subscribership, and may either increase or decrease the rival's price. The model presented in the Appendix B presents similar results for intensity of use: increases in the affiliate's quality increases both prices and increases aggregate intensity of use, while decreases in the rival's quality increases the affiliate's price, and decreases aggregate intensity of use.

B. Upstream Equilibrium

Having characterized the relationship between increased discrimination (or increased efficiency) and prices and output, we now turn to the question of the relationship between the degree of vertical integration and the amount of discrimination (or the efficiency gain). In this section, we demonstrate that some of the implications of the discrimination hypothesis for the relationship between observable measures of performance (such as price, quantity and quality) and the structural characteristics of the market differ from the implications of the efficiency hypothesis. Because there are cross-sectional differences in the degree of vertical integration across geographic areas in this industry, we can test these implications.

The key structural feature of the markets for the upstream input, land-line phone service, is that while each LEC is a monopolist over some area, those areas are not necessarily co-extensive with the

12

areas served by the cellular companies. In some markets, different portions of the market are served by different monopolist LECs. Fewer than 5% of the geographic markets (as delineated by the cellular licenses) are served by a single LEC providing local land-line service to all consumers. On average, about 3/4 of the end offices in a cellular market were owned by the largest LEC in the market, although the figure ranged from a low of 27% up to 100%. This suggests that the ability of the largest LEC to affect the quality of the unaffiliated cellular company will vary across markets. At the same time, as discussed in section II, in areas with multiple LECs, ownership of the affiliated cellular company is often shared among the LECs. For about 1/3 of the top 100 cellular markets in our sample (we only have equity ownership data for these 100) one LEC owned all of the equity in the affiliated cellular company. On average, the dominant LEC owned about 88% of the cellular company's equity, ranging down to a low of 28%.[19]

These cross-sectional differences allow for empirical examination of the importance of both the incentives to discrimination created by integration, and the efficiency effects of integration. In particular, if discriminatory incentives exist, they will be greatest in markets characterized by the dominant firm owning a large share of the equity in the cellular company, and also a large share of the land lines used for interconnection. Conversely, if integration lead to lower operating cost or higher quality for cellular affiliates (e.g, through reduced scope for opportunism), we would expect that such markets will have less expensive or higher quality cellular service.

i. The Discrimination Hypothesis

To formally analyze the relationship between ownership structure the incentive to discriminate, we consider the incentives of LECs. As noted above, each cellular market is served by one or more LECs, each a regulated monopolist over some portion of the geographic area covered by the cellular license. LEC j owns a fraction, α_j, of the facilities used to interconnect cellular end users to wireline end users in that cellular market, and a fraction, γ_j, of the equity interest in the affiliated cellular firm (firm B). The discrimination hypothesis is that LEC j can manipulate Z_A^j in order to advance the interests of its cellular affiliate. To isolate the effect of discrimination, we assume that there are no efficiencies from integration, so that Z_B^j is fixed. Since Z_B^j is fixed, we can parameterize quality as $Y_j = Z_B^j - Z_A^j$. Each LEC will choose its own profit maximizing level of quality degradation, Y_j, for cellular calls between customers in its service area and cellular firm A. We assume that the cellular companies are required to have

---

[19]One can think of these differences as difference in the degree of vertical integration in that the kinds of incentives created by integration are also created by owning a share of the equity in the cellular affiliate. The greater the ownership interest, the closer the relationship becomes to full integration.

common prices for calls between their customers and all wireline customers regardless of the LEC involved. These prices will be based on average quality across interconnecting LECs in the cellular market, $Y = \Sigma \alpha_j \, Y_j$.

The land-line monopolists are all regulated, which we interpret to mean that the monetary interconnection charge (W) is given, and cannot vary between the two downstream firms. To simplify the notation, assume that the monopolists' marginal costs of interconnection are zero. The demand facing monopolist j in its area is the derived demand from the two downstream firms, $q_i^j = q_i^j(P_A(Y,W), P_B(Y,W), Y_j)$, $i = A,B$. We write this demand in the reduced form, $q_i^j = q_i^j(Y_j, W, Y)$. Aggregate sales of each downstream firm is the sum of the sales in each portion of the cellular market; $q_i = \Sigma^j q_i^j$. Integrated firm j's profit is then

$$\Pi_j = W \left[q_B^j(W, Y, Y_j) + q_A^j(W, Y, Y_j) \right] + \gamma_j q_B(W, Y)(P_B(W, Y) - C).$$

Firm j's only decision variable is Y_j so that maximization yields

$$0 = \alpha_j \gamma_j \left[(P_B - C) \left(\frac{\partial q_B}{\partial Y} + \frac{\partial q_B}{\partial P_B} \frac{\partial P_B}{\partial Y} + \frac{\partial q_B}{\partial P_A} \frac{\partial P_A}{\partial Y} \right) + q_B \frac{\partial P_B}{\partial Y} \right] + W \left(\frac{dq_B^j}{dY_j} + \frac{dq_A^j}{dY_j} \right).$$

Cellular firm B's first-order condition with respect to price is $\partial q_B / \partial P_B (P_B - C) = -q_B$ so that firm j's first-order condition can be re-written

$$\gamma_j \alpha_j (P_B - C) \left(\frac{\partial q_B}{\partial Y} + \frac{\partial q_B}{\partial P_A} \frac{\partial P_A}{\partial Y} \right) = -W \left(\frac{dq_B^j}{dY_j} + \frac{dq_A^j}{dY_j} \right). \tag{6}$$

Equation (6) reflects a familiar logic. The left-hand side is the marginal profit the cellular affiliate gains from a reduction in its rival's quality, multiplied by firm j's share of those profits. The right hand side is the marginal effect of discrimination on the profits j earns from interconnection with cellular carriers.[20] Note that the left-hand side is increasing in γ. As Proposition 3 shows, if LEC j owns zero equity in the cellular company, then it has no incentive to discriminate.

_____

[20] In this model, the incentive to discriminate derives, at least in part, from the existence of price regulation. To see this, note that $\partial Y_j^* / \partial W < 0$ (where Y_j^* is LEC j's choice of Y_j) i.e., as the regulated price rises, the incentive to discriminate falls.

Proposition 3: If $\gamma_j = 0$, LEC j does not discriminate

Proof: Equation (6) implies that if $\gamma_j = 0$, LEC j chooses Y_j to maximize cellular phone use. From Proposition 2, we know that cellular use is decreasing in Y_j, so $Y_j = 0$ maximizes cellular phone use. ∎

Since, aggregated across LECs in a market, both ownership measures sum to one, this result does not directly address the question of interest here; how does the level of discrimination vary across markets? To translate this model into useful empirical implications, we need to consider how aggregate quality in a market varies with its structure (i.e., the distribution of α and γ among LECs). Proposition 4 addresses the question of how the concentration of ownership of LECs in a market affects the incentive to discriminate. In general, with multiple LECs in a market, each increases the profits of the affiliated cellular company when it degrades the non-affiliate's quality. If other LECs own shares of the affiliate's equity, then LEC j confers a positive externality on the other LECs when it degrades the non-affiliate's quality. The higher LEC j's share of the ownership of the affiliate, the smaller the externality (i.e., the greater the internalized benefit of the degradation). At the same time, more concentrated ownership of the land-lines increases an individual LEC's ability to degrade quality. Hence, higher concentration of both kinds increases discrimination.

To formalize this, we offer the following definition of increased concentration:

Definition: An *increase in concentration* occurs if a given percentage of assets (either financial or physical) is held by fewer firms, holding the ownership of the remaining percentage constant.

For example, we say that the concentration of financial assets is higher in market i than in market k if a $(1-\eta)$ share of the affiliate's equity is held by one LEC in market i, and two LECs in market k, while the composition of ownership in remaining η share is the same in both markets.

Proposition 4: Assume all LECs discriminate in equilibrium. Then, an increase in concentration increases the aggregate amount of discrimination.

Proof: Consider the profits of LECs 1 and 2 in a market with $n \geq 2$ LECs. The combined profits of these two firms are

$$\Pi_1 + \Pi_2 \equiv \Pi_L = W \sum_{i=1}^{2} \left(q_B^i(W,Y) + q_A^i(W,Y) \right) + (\gamma_1 + \gamma_2) q_B(W,Y) \left(P_B(W,Y) - C \right) \tag{7}$$

The change in Π_L when firm 1 increases Y_1 is

15

$$(\gamma_1+\gamma_2)\alpha_1(P_B-C)\left(\frac{\partial q_B}{\partial Y}+\frac{\partial q_B}{\partial P_A}\frac{\partial P_A}{\partial Y}\right)+W\left(\frac{dq_B}{dY_1}+\frac{dq_A}{dY_1}\right)=$$

$$(\gamma_1+\gamma_2)\alpha_1(P_B-C)\left(\frac{\partial q_B}{\partial Y}+\frac{\partial q_B}{\partial P_A}\frac{\partial P_A}{\partial Y}\right)+W\left(\frac{\partial q_B^1}{\partial Y_1}+\frac{\partial q_A^1}{\partial Y_1}\right)+ \tag{8}$$

$$\alpha_1\sum_{i=1}^{2}W\left[\frac{\partial P_B}{\partial Y}\left(\frac{\partial q_B^i}{\partial P_B}+\frac{\partial q_A^i}{\partial P_B}\right)+\frac{\partial P_A}{\partial Y}\left(\frac{\partial q_B^i}{\partial P_A}+\frac{\partial q_A^i}{\partial P_A}\right)\right]$$

While the change in LEC 1's profits is

$$\gamma_1\alpha_1(P_B-C)\left(\frac{\partial q_B}{\partial Y}+\frac{\partial q_B}{\partial P_A}\frac{\partial P_A}{\partial Y}\right)+W\left[\frac{\partial q_B^1}{\partial Y_1}+\frac{\partial q_A^1}{\partial Y_1}\right]+\alpha_1W\left[\frac{\partial P_B}{\partial Y}\left(\frac{\partial q_B^1}{\partial P_B}+\frac{\partial q_A^1}{\partial P_B}\right)+\frac{\partial P_A}{\partial Y}\left(\frac{\partial q_B^1}{\partial P_A}+\frac{\partial q_A^1}{\partial P_A}\right)\right] \tag{9}$$

The difference between expressions (8) and (9) represents the externality that increases in Y_1 generate for LEC 2. That difference equals

$$\alpha_1\gamma_2(P_B-C)\left(\frac{\partial q_B}{\partial Y}+\frac{\partial q_B}{\partial P_A}\frac{\partial P_A}{\partial Y}\right)+\alpha_1W\left[\frac{\partial P_B}{\partial Y}\left(\frac{\partial q_B^2}{\partial P_B}+\frac{\partial q_A^2}{\partial P_B}\right)\right] \tag{10}$$

Assuming there is an interior solution to equation (6) for firm 2, we know,

$$\gamma_2(P_B-C)\left(\frac{\partial q_B}{\partial Y}+\frac{\partial q_B}{\partial P_A}\frac{\partial P_A}{\partial Y}\right)+W\frac{\partial P_B}{\partial Y}\left(\frac{\partial q_B^2}{\partial P_B}+\frac{\partial q_A^2}{\partial P_B}\right)=-\frac{W}{\alpha_2}\left(\frac{\partial q_A^2}{\partial Y_2}+\frac{\partial q_B^2}{\partial Y_2}\right) \tag{6'}$$

Substituting (6') into (10), it follows that the externality is equal to $-(W/\alpha_2)\Sigma[(\partial q_B^2/\partial Y_2+\partial q_A^2/\partial Y_2)/]>$ 0. Similar analysis demonstrates that firm 2 will also choose a level of Y below that which maximizes Π_L. Hence, each firm will undersupply Y relative to the level which maximizes the joint profit of the two LECs. ∎

Proposition 4 establishes that when one firm controls an $(\alpha_1+\alpha_2)$ share of physical assets and a $(\gamma_1+\gamma_2)$ share of financial assets, aggregate discrimination is higher than when two separate firms each own γ_i (α_i) shares of the financial (physical) assets. The two effects are complementary in the sense that the higher the share of physical assets held by the largest LEC in the market, the greater the profitability of (and the greater the aggregate discrimination associated with) increasing its share of ownership in the cellular affiliate.

16

This suggests that the incentive to affect quality will vary across markets. Intuitively, discrimination reduces upstream profits, but increases cellular or *downstream* profits. The smaller the LEC's share of the affiliate's equity, the smaller the incentive to discriminate in order to increase the LEC's profits. Another way of seeing this is that the LEC ignores the positive externality it generates for other holders of equity in the affiliate, and hence under-discriminates compared to the level it would choose if it owned 100% of the equity.

Thus far, we have taken α and γ as exogenous. It seems reasonable to treat physical asset ownership as exogenous here; LECs had existing networks in place prior to the award of FCC cellular licenses, and these service areas would not change much in response to the initiation of cellular phone service. However, as discussed in section II, the composition of ownership in each B side cellular company was a joint decision of the LECs in each area (especially for large markets). Given the potential for side payments between LECs, a plausible assumption regarding the γ_j is that they were chosen to maximize joint profits. The complementarity between the incentives derived from concentrating α and γ suggests that markets with high concentration of physical assets will be characterized by greater concentration in ownership stake in the affiliate. In fact, it can be shown that as the concentration of physical asset ownership increases, the industry profit-maximizing concentration of financial assets increases as well. Hence, treating the γ_j as exogenous does not change the basic conclusion that, under the discrimination hypothesis, aggregate discrimination would be increasing in concentration.

ii. Efficiency Hypothesis

The efficiency hypothesis is that greater integration between LECs and cellular phone companies will reduce cellular company costs, and/or increase the quality of their product. Advocates of allowing regulated firms, such as LECs, to enter vertically-related unregulated businesses point to the potential efficiencies associated with such integration (see e.g., Alchian (1995)). Broadly speaking, the source of purported gains are economies of scope, which in turn derive from the ability to use some input more intensively. In the cellular phone context, for example, economies of scope might derive from the integrated firm having low incremental costs of adding additional lines (required to connect cellular transmitters) to existing wire lines along existing rights of way.

Of course, such economies can be realized by contract between unaffiliated cellular companies and LECs. Integration leads to efficiencies only to the extent that integration results in lower transaction cost than would a contract. Two kinds of transactions cost are relevant in this industry, and both are likely to be influenced by the structure of the upstream market. The first kind of transactions cost is simply the cost of negotiating with multiple parties. For example, to construct the wireline networks between transmitters, the cellular company will have to deal with every LEC providing interconnection in the area. As the number of such LECs in the market falls, the cellular company will have to deal with with fewer parties, and it seems reasonable that the cost of contracting (e.g., to add cells) will decline. This implies that greater concentration of α will be associated with lower transactions costs of creating a cellular network.

The second kind of transactions costs are those emphasized in the literature on the theory of the firm. In particular, the literature emphasizes that in many contractual relationships, there are assets whose value is significantly higher within that relationship than outside of it. Klein, Crawford, & Alchian (1978) refer to the difference between the values within and outside the relationship as the *appropriable quasi-rents* of the relationship. As Klein, Crawford, & Alchian and Grossman & Hart (1986) show, the existence of significant appropriable quasi-rents can lead both parties to act in ways inconsistent with maximizing joint profits (as they try to position themselves to obtain more of the quasi-rents). For example, Grossman and Hart show that inefficient initial investment can occur if the physical assets are owned by separate parties, leading ultimately to higher production costs than those that maximize joint profits. One way to mitigate their incentive is for one party to the contract to own a partial equity interest in the other party. This ownership interest increases a party's incentive to make investments that maximize joint profits (rather than increase their bargaining position).[21] The size of appropriable quasi-rents are particularly large in this industry because some of the investments made by the cellular company are highly specific to its relationship with the LEC (e.g., virtually worthless if the LEC discontinues services). It follows that since LECs with a greater γ will have more incentive to maximize joint profits, cellular companies in markets characterized by high γ will make more appropriate production decisions. For example, a cellular company which is 100% owned by a LEC will be more likely to invest in new transmission towers, because it knows that the LEC has appropriate incentives to promptly and efficiently provide connections between the new towers and the rest of the cellular network.

A related source of efficiencies from integration come about through a reduction in a type of double marginalization. One way to think about double marginalization is that the downstream firm chooses output to equate its marginal revenue and marginal cost, ignoring the upstream firm's (positive) marginal profit from an additional sale at the given wholesale price. Hence, actions by the downstream firm that increase output (e.g., reducing price, increasing quality) also increase joint profits, as long as the upstream firm earns a positive margin on its product. As with the transactions cost hypothesis, the predictions of this hypothesis are that the affiliated cellular company should have a lower price/ higher quality than its rival, and that output will be higher in markets with greater γ. Another prediction is that

---

[21] Hansen and Lott (1996) argue that partial ownership interests often serve to harmonize the incentives of the contracting parties.

the unaffiliated cellular company will have a greater incentive to use substitute inputs for interconnection. This latter prediction appears to be true, since, according to industry sources, unaffiliated cellular companies tend to build their own connections between their towers and switches, whereas the affiliated cellular companies lease a line from the LEC for this connection.

If the greater efficiency associated with higher γ led to lower costs of providing service of any specific quality, but did not change the costs of increasing quality, then under the efficiency hypothesis, we would expect greater concentration of ownership to reduce prices. Alternatively, if efficiency took the form of reducing the cost of providing quality, then we would expect a positive relationship between Z_B and γ or α, although prices could be higher in markets with greater integration. As discussed in Section II, one important means of increasing the quality of cellular service is through the addition of more cells. Therefore, if integration primarily affects the cost of adding cells, it is plausible that efficiency will be reflected in higher quality rather than lower prices.

iii. Empirical Implications

In section A, we described how changes in quality parameters, Z_B and Z_A, affect prices and quantity. We then showed how these quality parameters vary with market characteristics under the discrimination and efficiency hypotheses. The analysis demonstrated that under the discrimination hypothesis, higher concentration of physical asset ownership will lead to higher concentration of ownership of equity in cellular company B, and both types of concentration lead to lower quality for the affiliate's rival (greater discrimination). Combining this with the results from Proposition 2 on downstream effects of discrimination implies that quality and quantity will be lower in markets with high ownership concentration. Proposition 1 implies that affiliate prices would be higher in such markets, and non-affiliate prices may be higher.

The implications of the efficiency hypothesis are more ambiguous. However, if one is willing to assume that integration leads to higher quality, rather than lower production costs, the above analysis clearly predicts a positive relationship between the affiliate's quality and the ownership concentration measures. In this case, the efficiency hypothesis has some similar implications to the discrimination hypothesis in that both predict a positive relationship between ownership concentration and the quality difference between the cellular firms. Combining this conclusion with Proposition 1, we find that under either hypothesis, higher prices for both firms, and a greater difference between the two firms' prices will be associated with greater concentration of land-line ownership and equity ownership in the cellular company. The two hypotheses differ in their predictions regarding the effects of ownership concentration on quality and quantity. The efficiency hypothesis predicts that both quantity and quality will be higher in markets with higher ownership concentration.

One word of caution about these conclusions. The cost-shifting hypothesis discussed above yields similar empirical implications to the efficiency hypothesis. In this industry, cost-shifting may consist of the regulated firm making expenditures which increase the quality of cellular service, but where the cellular company does not contribute to covering those expenditures. This hypothesis yields similar implications to the efficiency hypothesis because if cost-shifting is occurring, then we would anticipate that the amount of cost-shifting would vary with the concentration of physical asset ownership and of equity ownership in the cellular carrier. Consequently, just as under the efficiency hypothesis, we would expect quality to be higher in markets with higher ownership concentration. It may be possible to distinguish this hypothesis from the efficiency hypothesis by testing whether land-line customers pay higher prices in markets with higher cellular service quality. We hope to examine this question in future research.

IV.   Description of Data

The models in section III predict some specific relationships between the ownership variables and observable market outcomes (i.e., price, quantity and quality). For example, the discrimination hypothesis predicts that the greater the share of the affiliate's equity held by the dominant LEC, the lower the quality of the affiliate's rival's service. The predicted relationships are based on other things being held constant. In particular, the predictions in Proposition 1 hold for a given set of demand and cost parameters. When this condition is not met, for example when there are differences in demand across markets, prices will vary across markets even if the predictions of Proposition 1 are correct (in terms of the models, these correspond to differences in θ or the distribution of X). To empirically evaluate the predictions of the alternative models, we need to account for cross-sectional differences in demand and cost. This section describes the dependent variables, the ownership variables of interest, and variables used to represent differences in cost or demand. Table 1 provides descriptions and sources for the data used and Table 2 provides some summary statistics.

Dependent Variables

As noted above, the models in section III describe how observable market outcomes change with the degree of vertical integration. Our price variables are calculated from posted cellular rates that were in effect in October 1991, as compiled by Information Enterprises, a former industry consulting firm. Rate indices were used rather than per-minute charges to reflect the non-linear nature of cellular pricing. Each cellular provider has a range of plans from which consumers can choose. These plans vary by levels of monthly access fees, the per-minute charges for peak and off-peak usage, and any minutes of peak or off-peak airtime that might be included in the monthly access fee. The average cost-per-minute of usage

20

depends on the particular plan a customer chooses, the average level of peak and off-peak usage, and the cellular provider's billing increment.[22]

Five rate indices were calculated for each retail plan provided by 560 cellular systems (generally, two in each city) offering cellular services in 293 metropolitan areas (CGSAs). The 293 CGSAs included in the study are drawn from the 306 metropolitan areas for which the FCC has granted cellular licenses. Thirteen CGSAs were dropped from the sample because some price data were unavailable.

In order to make rates comparable across different firms in different CGSAs, we made certain assumptions about average airtime usage. The five indices used were based on average usage of 100, 200, 300, 400 and 500 minutes per month. The indices were calculated on the assumptions that (1) 80% of usage was at peak rates and (2) the average length of each call was 2.5 minutes. We also assumed that consumers would know their average usage rate, and would therefore choose the particular plan that was most economical for their particular level of usage. Thus, for a given cellular provider with, say, five rate plans, if RI100 (the index for 100 minutes of airtime per month) was lowest for plan 2, then the plan 2 rate index was chosen as the appropriate dependent variable for regressions based on the RI100 index. If, for the same firm, plan 4 offered the lowest cost for using 200 minutes of airtime a month, then the 200 minute-per-month index for plan 4 was used as that firm's RI200 index.

Quantity measures were taken from the ServQuest survey conducted by Equifax NDS in 1995 and the Bill Harvesting II survey conducted by PNR and Associates in 1995. Both national surveys asked respondents, among other things, if they subscribed to cellular service and the size of their average bill. ServQuest included about 20,000 respondents while Bill Harvesting II included about 10,000 respondents. Responses were aggregated within cellular geographic markets to measure the quantity demanded as both the fraction of households in a market subscribing to cellular service and the average household cellular bill in a market.

Quality measures were constructed from the ServQuest survey. The ServQuest survey also asked respondents if they are satisfied with, or had a favorable opinion of, both their cellular provider and their land-line phone company. These were aggregated into the fraction of households satisfied or having a favorable opinion of their cellular and land-line companies. Two possible measurement error problems with these variables are that households in a particular area may tend to rate everything lower and that an affiliated cellular company can benefit from the LEC's reputation, especially if they share brand names.

---

[22] Longer billing increments lead to higher costs for any given level of average usage, holding per-minute charges constant. For example, a firm that bills in one minute increments will charge for two minutes of airtime if a call lasts one and one-half minutes while a firm that bills in one-half minute increments would charge the same call for just one and one-half minutes of airtime.

We attempt to alleviate these two potential problems by deflating the variables measuring the fraction of households satisfied with (or having favorable opinions of) their cellular provider by the fraction of household satisfied with (or having favorable opinions of) their LEC. Hence, our measure of "satisfaction" is the ratio of the percentage of housefholds satisfied with their cellular service, divided by the percentage "satisfied" with LEC.

Ownership Variables

The two relevant ownership variables are the fraction of the affiliated cellular company's equity held by the dominant LEC (equity ownership) and the fraction of land-line phones in a market for which the integrated LEC supplies interconnection (physical asset ownership). The equity stake in the cellular company is taken from an annual market analysis report on the cellular industry produced by Donaldson, Lufkin and Jenrette, which lists the ownership shares in both licenses in each of the top 100 markets.[23] The percent of interconnecting land-line phones served by the dominant LEC is approximated by the percent of end office switches owned by the integrated LEC. Bellcore's Local Exchange Routing Guide (LERG) contains ownership and interconnection information for each of the more than 30,000 telephone company switches in North America. These data are updated monthly and are usually used by network engineers to plan call paths. Among other switch information, the LERG identifies the owner, location and type of each switch. We matched each switch by zipcode to the geographic cellular markets[24] to calculate the share of end office switches owned by the dominate LEC in each geographic area. One potentially serious source of measurement error in this variable stems from the heterogeneity of end office switches. The affiliated LECs tend to operate in the more densely populated urban areas where each end office tends to serve more telephone lines. Thus, the share of end offices owned by the affiliated LEC will tend to underestimate the share of land-line customers it serves.

The other variable created from LERG data is the percentage of tandem switches owned by the dominant LEC. Telephone traffic terminating beyond the end office is typically routed through a tandem switch. Likewise, interconnection between different companies' networks (long distance, cellular, neighboring LECs) typically occurs at a tandem switch. If all of the LECs in an area interconnect to cellular companies through the dominant LEC's tandem switches, then the dominant LEC can effectively discriminate on all calls requiring interconnection. Holding this effect constant, the fraction of end offices owned by the dominant LEC is likely to proxy for possible efficiencies to vertical integration.

---

[23]Actually, we were unable to construct the ownership variable for three of the 100 markets. We would like to thank Karim Zia at Donaldson, Lufkin, & Jenrette for making these data available.

[24]The match rate was about 98%.

Demand- and Cost-Related Factors

Six demand-related exogenous variables are included in the regression equations. These are: per capita income in each metropolitan area; the population of each metropolitan area; per capita state employment in finance, insurance, and real estate; vehicle miles per capita by state; a qualitative measure of freeway congestion in each metropolitan area compiled by the Federal Highway Administration; and the average time spent commuting to work in each metropolitan area as determined by the U.S. census. The last three variables are included to account for the frequent use of cellular telephone service by users of cellular car phones. Employment in finance, insurance, and real estate is intended to capture demand by measuring employment in industries that might have greater than average demands for cellular service. We anticipate that demand, hence price and quantity, will be increasing in these demand variables.

Three cost-related exogenous variables could help explain differences in cellular markets.[25] The median housing price in each metropolitan area is used as a measure of relative land values across the metropolitan areas, which can be a factor affecting the costs of installing base stations. This can also be a proxy for a cost-of-living index,[26] that might arguably affect cellular rates as a factor of both demand and supply. Since the cellular telephone industry is relatively young, it is likely that it exhibits learning-by-doing, as information about efficient production techniques is obtained only through experience. To account for this possibility, the price regressions include a variable for the number of months that each system was in operation, to proxy for declining marginal costs due to learning-by-doing. Finally, since taxes vary across states and localities, we include a cost variable equal to the sum of the marginal tax rates of state corporate income taxes, sales taxes, excise taxes, and other taxes that apply to cellular providers.

V. Empirical Results

The issues of primary interest are the relationships between the degree of vertical integration and market outcomes (price, quantity, and quality). These relationships could be estimated in a structural (i.e., demand and supply) model. However, structural estimates often require strong *a priori* behavioral restrictions. Because structural parameters are not our primary interest, we instead restrict our attention to reduced form regressions of price, quantity and quality on variables measuring the degree of vertical

---

[25]Another relevant aspect of costs are the access fees that cellular systems pay to the local wireline telephone company in order to connect cellular calls to the wireline system. (See Kaestner and Kahn (1990)). However, consistent measures of access charges are not available.

[26]The consumer price index (CPI) is available by MSA, but only for relatively large MSAs. Using median housing prices as a measure of the cost of living rather than the CPI allows us to include many smaller cities and some states, and reduce sample selection biases.

integration and demand and cost variables. Two aspects of the degree of vertical integration, the variables of interest, are included as regressors in the equations explaining these variables. Estimates generally indicate a positive relationship between the degree of vertical integration and prices. The estimated relationship between integration and quality/quantity is more complex. We have two measures of ownership of physical assets, and the coefficients on the two measures are generally opposite in sign and similar in magnitude. It is plausible that tandem switch ownership measures the ability to discriminate, while end office ownership measures the scope for vertical efficiencies. In this case, our results are consistent with vertical integration leading to both more efficient production and a greater scope for discrimination.

Table 3 reports reduced form price equation results using an Aitken estimator to control for heteorskedasticity.[27] The first two columns present results for the largest 100 markets for which cellular company equity share data exist,[28] while the next two columns present results based on all available markets. Price data for the five calling volume levels were pooled with dummy variables included in the regressions for each plan.[29] Column (1) and (3) represent regressions using the 'A' license, or unaffiliated, cellular company price, while columns (2) and (4) use represent the 'B' license, or affiliated, company price. In the top 100 markets, those markets with a higher degree of financial ownership of the cellular company by the dominant LEC have higher prices in both licensee regressions. End office concentration is associated with higher affiliated cellular company prices only. In addition, coefficients for the unaffiliated company are smaller than the respective coefficients for the affiliated company in all specifications. The financial ownership effects are not only statistically significant but also economically meaningful; an increase in the LEC's ownership of the cellular company's equity of 20% (e.g., from 40 to 50%), increases the affiliate's prices by nearly 5%. These results are not consistent with vertical integration leading to cost-saving. As Proposition 1 indicates, the results are consistent with both the hypothesis that integration led to higher quality and that integration leads to discrimination. When the sample is expanded but the cellular company's equity variable is dropped, we find no statistically significant relationship between any of the physical asset ownership variables and price. Coefficients on demand and cost generally have the expected sign or are not statistically significant.

---

[27]OLS results are qualitatively similar. For a discussion of theTwo Staged Aitken estimator, see Johnston (1984), p. 303.

[28]Since some element of the data was not available for three observations, these regressions represent 85 separate geographic markets for 'A' licenses and 88 for 'B' licenses.

[29]Estimating the five volume prices separately yields qualitatively similar coefficients, but, as expected, larger standard errors.

Another implication of both the discrimination and the efficiency hypotheses is that price difference between the A and B licensees should increase with the degree of vertical integration Table 4 reports regressions of this price difference regressed against ownership measures. The regressions do not include the available independent variables measuring differences in demand and costs because those variables measure market characteristics common to both cellular companies. However, because the dependent variable is the price difference, the regression controls for any market-level effects on demand and costs omitted from the price level regressions. This provides a means of determining the importance of omitted variables, such as access charges. The results mimic those in table 3 in that price differences increase with both cellular company equity integration and end office ownership, with the first effect being much larger, and that there is no discernable ownership effect in the expanded sample. The fraction of tandem ownership tends to decrease the price difference in the top 100 markets, but this effect is much smaller than the others and is significant at the 5% level, rather than the 1% level of the other two variables. While these regressions do not distinguish between the discrimination and efficiency hypotheses, they do tend to support the vertical differentiation model. Specifically, that model implies that efficiency and discrimination both lead to the price effects observed in tables 3 and 4 (e.g., the affiliate's price increases more with financial ownership than does its competitor's price).

To distinguish between the discrimination hypothesis and the hypothesis that efficiencies led to higher quality, it is necessary to examine the relationship between ownership and measures of quality and quantity. Table 5 reports regression results for total transaction quantity in a market from the ServQuest survey; individual firm data were not available. Columns (1) and (3) report regression results using the fraction of households subscribing to cellular service as the dependent variable, which corresponds to the "extensive margin" model discussed in Section III and Appendix A. Columns (2) and (4) use average monthly expenditures as the dependent variable, and hence correspond to the "intensive margin" model discussed in Appendix B. Since the construction of these variables induces heteroskedasticity, observations are weighted by the number of households in the market.[30] The obvious limitation of the expenditure variable is that it confounds the effects of quantity and price. In the intensive margin model, efficiencies which increase quality increase both the quantity purchased and the total expenditure of each consumer. Discrimination decreases quantity and has an ambiguous effect on total expenditure. As a result, an increase in total expenditure would be consistent with both explanations, while a decrease would

---

[30]For example, the variable measuring the fraction of households subscribing will have a smaller standard error in markets where more respondents answered the survey. Since the survey attempted to be nationally representative, the number of respondents is roughly proportional to the number of households.

be consistent only with the discrimination hypothesis.

The two physical ownership measures are generally statistically significant in these regressions; subscribership and expenditures per household are increasing in end-office ownership and decreasing in tandem ownership. These effects are typically similar in magnitude, so a simultaneous, equal-sized increase in both forms of ownership would have little effect on either quantity measure.[31] An increase in tandem ownership reduces expenditures and subscribership, effects which are consistent with the discrimination hypothesis. Conversely, an increase in end-office ownership increases subscribership (despite higher prices), as suggested by the efficiency hypothesis. One potential interpretation of these results is that an increase in tandem switch ownership (the essential interconnection facility) does not lead to efficiencies, but rather enables the dominant firm to reduce the quality of cellular company A's service. Conversely, the positive signs on the percentage of end-offices variables suggests that there are efficiencies from coordination; a more extensive phone network reduces cellular company B's cost of negotiating interconnections and/or obtaining locations to construct transmitters, and hence reduces B's cost of creating a higher quality network.

Other demand and cost variables generally have the expected sign, or are not statistically significant. The exceptions to this are FIRE employment, commute time and housing prices. One interpretation of the positive coefficient on housing prices is that in addition to measuring marginal costs as we initially thought, housing prices are a demand shifter; e.g., housing prices reflect wealth in a way not reflected in per-capita income. Estimated coefficient values are qualitatively unchanged between the two samples, but standard errors tend to decrease with the larger sample size.

Table 6 represents the same regression equations as table 5, replacing the dependent variables constructed from the ServQuest data with those from the Bill Harvesting II data. As noted above, the Bill Harvesting II data contains fewer observations, and we therefore anticipate less precise coefficient estimates than in table 5. We have included the regression results for this data set primarily to test the robustness of the results in table 5. As anticipated, the standard errors of the coefficients are larger and, because the sample includes no cellular subscribers in smaller markets, the sample of markets included in the expenditures regressions is greatly reduced. Nevertheless, the ownership variables generally confirm the results found in table 5. One difference is that the magnitude of the tandem switch ownership coefficient is less than half that for the end office variable.

---

[31]These results do not appear to be the result of possible multicollinearity between the dominant firm's fraction of end offices and the fraction of tandem switches. The correlation between the two is less than 0.5 and deleting one does not appreciably change the coefficient of the other. Leamer (1978, at 170-81) suggests that when prior information on other variables does not significantly affect the parameter estimate of interest, the interpretation problem caused by multicollinearity is not severe.

Table 7 presents regression results on the subjective quality measures. Since the quality measures are based on subjective perceptions of cellular phone service, some care is required interpreting the results. In particular, the "favorable" or "satisfied" measures may reflect both "quality" and price, in that, holding "quality" constant, fewer consumers are likely to be satisfied in markets with higher prices. Hence, if we observe a higher percentage of consumers with "satisfactory" or "favorable" perceptions of their cellular service in markets with greater integration (despite the higher prices in such markets), then we would conclude that integration increases quality. If, however, price increases with integration, but satisfaction seems to be unaffected by integration, then it would indicate that quality rose with integration, but that increase was offset by the higher price. Finally, evidence that satisfaction declined with integration would support the discrimination hypothesis, and may mean greater integration is associated with both lower quality and higher prices.

As was the case for quantity, we only have observations on average quality for both cellular companies in each geographic area. Columns (1) and (3) report regression results using the ratio of respondents who view cellular service 'favorably' to those who view LEC service 'favorably' as the dependent variable, while columns (2) and (4) use a similar measure for respondents 'satisfied' with the service as the dependent variable. Again, correcting for heteroskedasticity resulting from the construction of these variables requires weighted OLS. The results are quite similar to the quantity results. Again, the two physical ownership measures are generally statistically significant and of opposite sign; favorable perceptions of quality of cellular service are increasing in end-office ownership and decreasing in tandem ownership. These effects are typically similar in magnitude, so a simultaneous, equal-sized increase in both forms of ownership would have little effect on either quality measure. Except for FIRE and income, demand and cost coefficients tend have the expected sign or are not statistically significant. Estimated coefficient values are qualitatively unchanged between samples, but standard errors tend to decrease with the larger sample size.

VI.   Conclusion

Despite the existence of a significant economic literature concerning the effects of vertical integration by a regulated entity, there is scant empirical evidence on the magnitude of these effects. To examine the empirical relevance of these theories, we study the cellular phone industry, an industry which has several features that make for a useful natural experiment. In this industry, the degree of vertical integration between the regulated monopolist and its unregulated affiliate varies exogenously across geographic areas. We find that the degree of integration has an economically and statistically significant impact on prices, quantity, and quality of cellular phone service. These results provide some evidence that these theories apply to the cellular phone industry and that they may apply to other regulated industries.

Estimation results also indicate that a relatively clear picture of an industry emerged only from series of related reduced form regressions. In contrast, the effects of vertical integration were not readily apparent in any single set of regression results. For example, looking at the price regressions alone might suggest that integration leads to discrimination, because greater integration was associated with higher prices. However, the quality and quantity regression suggest a more complex relationship, since greater subscribership was associated with higher levels of one of our two measures of physical asset integration. In general, incorrect inferences could be drawn from a single reduced form regression (e.g., price or quantity) if product quality is also endogenously determined.

Perhaps surprisingly, the results suggest no clear policy implications for cellular service. Integration in this industry appears to have resulted in both efficiencies and discrimination against the affiliate's competitor of roughly similar magnitude and opposite in sign. Our findings neither suggest that a prohibition against integration in this industry is clearly warranted, nor that such a prohibition would clearly harm consumers. Our results do suggest that concerns about discrimination in this industry are legitimate. Despite the presence of firewalls between the LEC and the affiliated cellular provider, the financial incentives created by equity ownership seem to have an effect on the LEC's behavior towards its affiliate and the affiliate's competitor. Likewise, our results suggest that LECs may be more efficient in producing products related to local telephone service. Line-of-business restrictions against LEC entry into related markets may deny consumers products from the most efficient producer.

References

Alchian, Armen, "Vertical Integration and Regulation in the Telephone Industry" in Higgins, Richard and Paul Rubin eds., <u>Deregulating Telecommunications</u> (N.Y: John Wiley and Sons), 1995, p. 44-9

Beard, T. Randolph, David Kaserman and John Mayo, "A Theoretical Analysis of Vertical Reintegration Under the Telecommunications Act of 1996," paper presented at the 1996 TPRC.

Bowman, Ward S. Jr., "Tying Arrangements and the Leveraging Problem" <u>Yale Law Journal</u>, 67 (1957) 19-36.

Brennan, Timothy, "Regulated Firms in Unregulated Markets: Understanding the Divestiture in <u>U.S. v AT&T</u>," <u>Antitrust Bulletin</u>, 32 (1987), 61-.

Calhoun, George, <u>Digital Cellular Radio</u> (Norwood, MA: Artech House), 1988.

Economides, Nicholas "The Incentive for Non-Price Discrimination by an Input Monopolist," Discussion Paper # 486, Center for Economic Policy Research, Stanford University, April, 1997.

Grossman, Sanford, J. and Hart, Oliver D., "The Costs and Benefits of Ownership: A Theory of Vertical Integration," <u>Journal of Political Economy</u> 94 (1986) 691-719.

Hansen, Robert G. and John R. Lott Jr., "Externalities and Corporate Objectives in a World with Diversified Shareholders/Consumers" <u>Journal of Financial and Quantitative Analysis</u>, 31 (1996), 43-68.

Johnston, John <u>Econometric Methods</u> 3rd Editon (New York, NY: McGraw-Hill), 1984.

Joskow, Paul L., "Vertical Integration and Long-Term Contracts: The Case of Coal-burning Electricity Generating Plants" <u>Journal of Law, Economics and Organization</u>, 1 (Spr, 85), 33-80.

Kaesther, Robert and Kahn, Brenda, "The Effects of Regulation and Competition on the Price of AT&T Intrastate Telephone Service," <u>Journal of Regulatory Economics</u> 2, 1990, 363-377.

Klein, Benjamin, Crawford, Robert and Alchian, Armen, "Vertical Integration, Appropriable Rents, and the Competitive Contracting Process," <u>Journal of Law and Economics</u> 21 (1978) 297-326.

Leamer, Edward, <u>Specification Searches</u> (N.Y: John Wiley and Sons), 1978.

McChesney, Fred S., "Empirical Tests of the Cross-subsidy and Discriminatory-access Hypotheses in Vertically Integrated Telephony," in Higgins, Richard and Paul Rubin eds., <u>Deregulating Telecommunications</u> (N.Y: John Wiley and Sons), 1995, p. 217-29.

Noll, Roger G. and Bruce D. Owen, "The Anticompetitive uses of Regulation: U.S. vs. AT&T": in John E. Kwoka and Lawrence J. White eds. <u>The Antitrust Revolution</u> (Glenview, IL: Scott, Foresman & Co.) 1989, pp. 290-337

Perry, Martin, "Vertical Integration" in Schmalensee and Willig eds., <u>The Handbook of Industrial Organization</u>

Posner, Richard, "Natural Monopoly and its Regulation," <u>Stanford Law Review</u> 21 (1969), 615-43.

Rosston, Gregory L., <u>An Economic Analysis of the Effects of FCC Regulation on Land Mobile Radio</u> Ph.d Dissertation, Stanford University (1994).

Shaked, Avner and John Sutton, "Relaxing Price Competition Through Product Differentiation" <u>Review of Economic Studies</u>, 49 (1982) 3-13.

Sibley, David and Weisman, Dennis, "The Competitive Incentives of Vertically Integrated Local Exchange Carriers: An Economic and Policy Analysis," <u>Journal of Policy Analysis and Management</u> (forthcoming, 1997).

Table 1
Data Sources

Variables	Source	Year
Dependent Variables		
Cellco Price	Cellular Price and Marketing Database (CPMD), Information Enterprises	1991
Cellco Subscribership, Avg. Bill	ServQuest Survey, Equifax NDS	1995
Cellco Subscribership, Avg. Bill	Bill Harveting II, PNR and Associates	1995
Satisfactied, Favorable Opinion	ServQuest Survey, Equifax NDS	1995
Ownership Variables		
Ownership of End Offices	Local Exchange Routing Guide (LERG), Bellcore	1996
Ownership of Tandem Offices	Local Exchange Routing Guide (LERG), Bellcore	1996
Ownership of Cellco Equity	Cellular Ownership Report, Donaldson, Lufkin & Jenrette	1995[32]
Demand Variables		
Income	Survey of Current Business, BEA	1991
Population	State and Metropolitan Area Data Book, U.S. Census Bureau	1991
Finance, Insurance and Real Estate Employment per Capita	Employment and Earnings, BLS	1991
Vehicles Miles per Capita	Selected Highway Statistics and Charts, FHA	1991
Freeway Congestion	FHA	1991
Average Commute Time	1990 Census of Population and Housing, U.S. Census	1990
Cost Variables		
Median Housing Price	FHA Trends of Home Mortgage Characteristics, HUD	1991
Marginal Tax Rate	State and Local Taxation of the Cellular Industry, CTIA	1991
Months of Cellco Operation	Cellular Telephone Industry Association (CTIA)	1991

---

[32] As modified to reflect PacTel's Divestiture of its Cellular Phone Asset.

Table 2
Summary Statistics - Means (Standard Deviations)

Variables	Top 100 Markets		Top 100 Markets		All Markets		All Markets	
	License A		License B		License A		License B	
Firm-Specific Variables								
Price 100 Minutes	58.01	(13.43)	59.99	(13.42)	56.05	(12.51)	58.41	(12.72)
Price 200 Minutes	92.29	(18.69)	93.75	(22.52)	89.36	(18.07)	91.20	(19.92)
Price 300 Minutes	124.06	(25.46)	126.77	(29.96)	119.95	(24.27)	122.12	(26.38)
Price 400 Minutes	154.87	(31.80)	158.25	(38.91)	150.24	(31.62)	151.64	(34.35)
Price 500 Minutes	182.92	(39.47)	189.44	(46.95)	177.75	(39.94)	180.69	(42.62)
Market Specific Variables								
ServQuest Subs. (%)	17.0		(1.8)		16.0		(1.9)	
ServQuest Avg. Bill	45.43		(4.63)		46.64		(4.56)	
Bill Harv. Subs. (%)	13.6		(8.0)		12.2		(14.0)	
Bill Harv. Avg. Bill	47.36		(26.97)		43.66		(24.99)	
Celco/Telco Favor.	0.811		(0.032)		0.810		(0.034)	
Celco/Telco Satisfied	0.829		(0.051)		0.817		(0.052)	
Cellco Equity (%)	84.7		(18.7)					
End Office (%)	73.8		(17.7)		69.7		(20.0)	
Tandem Switch (%)	71.3		(26.6)		77.6		(26.9)	
Income ($1,000)	17.88		(3.31)		16.41		(3.14)	
Popl. (1,000,000)	1.34		(1.51)		0.61		(1.06)	
FIRE Empl. (%)	2.79		(2.59)		2.49		(2.36)	
Veh. Miles (1,000)	8.72		(0.98)		8.85		(0.96)	
Freeway Congestion	2.85		(0.79)		2.15		(0.98)	
Commute Time	21.15		(2.90)		19.09		(2.90)	
House Price ($1,000)	77.9		(23.8)		68.8		(20.6)	
Tax Rate	12.5		(5.8)		13.0		(5.4)	

Table 3
Price Regression Results

Variables	Top 100 Markets		All Markets	
	A License	B License	A License	B License
Cellco Ownership	0.127* (0.045)	0.236* (0.054)		
End Office Ownership	0.029 (0.067)	0.205* (0.071)	-0.073 (0.044)	-0.013 (0.041)
Tandem Switch Ownership	-0.049 (0.036)	-0.041 (0.042)	0.001 (0.030)	0.024 (0.029)
Log Income	-0.114^{+} (0.056)	-0.015 (0.073)	0.069 (0.047)	0.154* (0.045)
Log Population	-0.035^{+} (0.016)	-0.033 (0.023)	-0.029^{+} (0.013)	-0.033^{+} (0.014)
Log FIRE Employment	0.030* (0.011)	0.048* (0.012)	0.018^{+} (0.008)	-0.001 (0.007)
Log Vehicle Miles	-0.184^{+} (0.093)	-0.164 (0.104)	-0.280* (0.071)	-0.379* (0.066)
Freeway Congestion	0.029^{+} (0.012)	0.038* (0.014)	0.034* (0.010)	0.045* (0.009)
Log Commute Time	0.253* (0.095)	0.127 (0.107)	0.201* (0.074)	0.190* (0.072)
Log Housing Price	0.292* (0.041)	0.263* (0.045)	0.123* (0.022)	0.091* (0.021)
Log Tax Rate	0.087* (0.017)	0.015 (0.022)	0.037* (0.014)	0.023^{+} (0.014)
Log Month of Operation	-0.018 (0.021)	0.104 (0.080)	-0.036^{+} (0.016)	-0.021 (0.029)
Observations	420	435	905	1000
R^2	.884	.828	.812	.801

To account for heteroskedasticity, an Aitken estimator was used. An intercept term and dummy variables for each calling volume plan were included in regressions but are not reported. Standard errors are in parentheses. A plus sign indicates statistical significance at the 10% level and an asterisk indicates the 1% level.

Table 4
Price Difference Regression Results
(Affiliate Price minus Independent Firm Price)

Variables	Top 100 Markets	All Markets
Cellco Ownership	18.90* (2.88)	
End Office Ownership	11.93* (3.58)	2.71 (2.19)
Tandem Switch Ownership	-5.07[+] (2.24)	1.30 (1.52)
Observations	445	935
R^2	.140	.004

An intercept term and dummy variables for each calling volume plan were included in regressions but are not reported. Standard errors are in parentheses. A plus sign indicates statistical significance at the 10% level and an asterisk indicates the 1% level.

Table 5
ServQuest Quantity Regression Results

Variables	Top 100 Markets		All Markets	
	Cellular Subscribership	Cellular Expenditures per Capita	Cellular Subscribership	Cellular Expenditures per Capita
Intercept	-1.025* (0.168)	-67.557* (17.737)	-0.956* (0.109)	-61.915* (12.628)
Cellco Ownership	-0.002 (0.009)	1.189 (0.915)		
End Office Ownership	0.021+ (0.009)	1.042 (0.908)	0.016* (0.005)	0.262 (0.587)
Tandem Switch Ownership	-0.016* (0.005)	-1.774* (0.582)	-0.012* (0.004)	-1.005+ (0.412)
Log Income	0.068* (0.011)	2.185+ (1.127)	0.072* (0.007)	3.828* (0.765)
Log Population	0.003 (0.002)	0.822* (0.231)	0.003+ (0.001)	0.861* (0.154)
Log FIRE Employment	-0.002 (0.002)	0.081 (0.177)	-0.002 (0.001)	0.023 (0.117)
Log Vehicle Miles	0.050 (0.013)	3.006+ (1.356)	0.044* (0.008)	2.180+ (0.967)
Freeway Congestion	0.004 (0.005)	-0.013 (0.548)	0.005+ (0.003)	-0.097 (0.350)
Log Commute Time	-0.040* (0.012)	-6.275* (1.276)	-0.038* (0.008)	-6.027* (0.919)
Log Housing Price	0.014+ (0.006)	5.131* (0.637)	0.009+ (0.004)	3.866* (0.408)
Log Tax Rate	0.002 (0.003)	-0.504+ (0.267)	0.002 (0.002)	-0.401+ (0.197)
Observations	89	89	198	198
R^2	.658	.710	.647	.662

To account for heteroskedasticity, observations are weighted by population. Standard errors are in parentheses. A plus sign indicates statistical significance at the 10% level and an asterisk indicates the 1% level.

Table 6
Bill Harvesting Quantity Regression Results

Variables	Top 100 Markets		All Markets	
	Cellular Subscribership	Cellular Expenditures per Capita	Cellular Subscribership	Cellular Expenditures per Capita
Intercept	-1.678$^+$ (0.884)	-166.033* (58.317)	-1.410$^+$ (0.692)	-161.248* (48.823)
Cellco Ownership	-0.023 (0.046)	0.373 (3.039)		
End Office Ownership	0.156* (0.045)	7.224$^+$ (2.915)	0.151* (0.032)	6.441* (2.301)
Tandem Switch Ownership	-0.060$^+$ (0.029)	-4.366$^+$ (1.937)	-0.073* (0.023)	-4.300* (1.592)
Log Income	-0.086 (0.057)	-7.758$^|$ (3.946)	-0.058 (0.042)	-5.485$^+$ (3.104)
Log Population	0.022$^+$ (0.012)	1.340 (0.785)	0.013 (0.008)	0.766 (0.604)
Log FIRE Employment	0.000 (0.009)	0.837 (0.600)	0.003 (0.007)	1.115$^+$ (0.475)
Log Vehicle Miles	0.247* (0.068)	19.867* (4.394)	0.203* (0.054)	18.870* (3.727)
Freeway Congestion	-0.008 (0.027)	-2.184 (1.181)	-0.002 (0.019)	-2.563$^+$ (1.410)
Log Commute Time	0.059 (0.064)	1.814 (4.077)	0.037 (0.050)	1.433 (3.474)
Log Housing Price	-0.012 (0.034)	3.541$^+$ (2.205)	-0.006 (0.023)	2.780$^+$ (1.581)
Log Tax Rate	-0.008 (0.013)	-0.891 (0.860)	-0.013 (0.011)	-1.209 (0.736)
Observations	87	81	195	142
R^2	.344	.356	.219	.259

To account for heteroskedasticity, observations are weighted by population. Standard errors are in parentheses. A plus sign indicates statistical significance at the 10% level and an asterisk indicates the 1% level.

Table 7
Surveyed Quality Regression Results

Variables	Top 100 Markets		All Markets	
	Ratio of Cellular to LEC 'Favorable'	Ratio of Cellular to LEC 'Satisfied'	Ratio of Cellular to LEC 'Favorable'	Ratio of Cellular to LEC 'Satisfied'
Intercept	0.398 (0.333)	0.351 (0.493)	0.425* (0.222)	0.349 (0.332)
Cellco Ownership	0.009 (0.017)	0.026 (0.025)		
End Office Ownership	0.032+ (0.017)	0.055+ (0.025)	0.025+ (0.010)	0.039+ (0.015)
Tandem Switch Ownership	-0.034* (0.011)	-0.064* (0.016)	-0.027* (0.007)	-0.048* (0.011)
Log Income	-0.044+ (0.021)	-0.099* (0.031)	-0.031+ (0.013)	-0.059* (0.020)
Log Population	0.005 (0.004)	0.016+ (0.006)	0.005+ (0.003)	0.017* (0.004)
Log FIRE Employment	0.009+ (0.003)	0.010+ (0.005)	0.007* (0.002)	0.008* (0.003)
Log Vehicle Miles	0.057+ (0.025)	0.057 (0.038)	0.050* (0.017)	0.045+ (0.025)
Freeway Congestion	-0.006 (0.010)	-0.003 (0.015)	-0.005 (0.006)	-0.004 (0.009)
Log Commute Time	-0.077* (0.024)	-0.151* (0.035)	-0.074* (0.016)	-0.149* (0.024)
Log Housing Price	0.038* (0.012)	0.096* (0.018)	0.030* (0.007)	0.073* (0.011)
Log Tax Rate	0.001 (0.005)	-0.002 (0.007)	0.001 (0.003)	-0.001 (0.005)
Observations	89	89	198	198
R^2	.438	.509	.343	.415

To account for heteroskedasticity, observations are weighted by population. Standard errors are in parentheses. A plus sign indicates statistical significance at the 10% level and an asterisk indicates the 1% level.

Appendix A - A Generalized Extensive Margin Model

In this appendix, we generalize the model in the text by allowing variation in θ_i (consumer i's reservation value for the good). Although a fully generalized model would allow for a continuum of θ_i, the important properties of that model are contained in a simpler model in which θ_i takes on one of two values. The reason that considering only two values of θ is sufficient to capture the heterogeneity is that for any given θ, consumers will segment themselves on the basis on their x_i in one of two ways. Hence, if we allow sufficient heterogeneity that some consumers fall into each category, then we have captured the essential feature of the more general model.

Specifically, for a given θ, one possibility is that consumers with x_i sufficiently high will buy from firm B (the high-quality firm), those with slightly lower x_i will buy from firm A, and those with the lowest x_i will not buy the good at all. The other possibility is that consumer with a specific θ and sufficiently high x_i will buy from firm B, and other consumers will not buy the good at all. That is, when θ is `large', the consumer with the lowest $x_i$ that buys from firm B is (almost) indifferent between firms A and B, while when $\theta$ is `small' B's lowest x_i customer is (almost) indifferent between firm B and not buying the good at all. No consumers of the latter type buy from firm A at all.[33]

Formally, assume consumer i values the good at $x_i Z_B + \theta_i$, where θ_i can take on one of two values; either $\theta_i = \theta_1$ or $\theta_i = \theta_2$ where $\theta_1 > \theta_2$. As in the text, we assume that x_i is uniformly distributed with support $(0,1)$, for both θ_1 and θ_2 consumers. Finally, let the percentage of consumers for whom $\theta_i = \theta_1$ be ρ. Then, we can write firm B's sales as

$$q_B = \rho \int_{\frac{P_B - P_A}{Z_B - Z_A}}^{1} dx + (1-\rho) \int_{\frac{P_B - \theta_2}{Z_B}}^{1} dx = \rho \left(1 - \frac{P_B - P_A}{Z_B - Z_A} \right) + (1-\rho) \left(1 - \frac{P_B - \theta_2}{Z_B} \right) \tag{A.1}$$

B's objective function is

$$\Pi_B = \left[\rho \left(1 - \frac{P_B - P_A}{Z_B - Z_A} \right) + (1-\rho) \left(1 - \frac{P_B - \theta_2}{Z_B} \right) \right] (P_B - C)$$

_____

[33] θ must be small in the sense that all consumers who prefer A's product to B's prefer no product to either firms' product. This requires

$$\frac{P_B - \theta}{Z_B} > \frac{P_B - P_A}{Z_B - Z_A}, \ so \ that \ \theta < P_B - \frac{Z_B}{Z_B - Z_A}(P_B - P_A).$$

A1

and its best-response function is

$$P_B(P_A) = \frac{\rho Z_B P_A + (Z_B - Z_A)(Z_B + C + (1-\rho)\theta_2) + \rho Z_A C}{2(Z_B + \rho Z_A - Z_A)}.$$ (A.2)

A's objective function is a multiple (ρ) of equation 5 of the simpler model in the text, so that its best-response function remains

$$P_A(P_B) = \frac{(P_B - \theta_1)Z_A}{2Z_B} + \frac{C + \theta_1}{2}.$$

Solving equations (A.1) and (A.2) simultaneously, we find

$$P_A^* = \left[\frac{2(Z_B - Z_A)\left(Z_B + C + (1-\rho)\theta_2 + \frac{\rho\theta_1}{2}\right) + 2\rho C(Z_B + Z_A) - \theta_1(4Z_B - 4Z_a + 3\rho Z_A)}{4Z_B - 4Z_A + 3\rho Z_A} \right] \frac{Z_A}{2Z_B} + \frac{C + \theta_1}{2},$$

$$P_B^* = \frac{2(Z_B - Z_A)\left(Z_B + C + (1-\rho)\theta_2 + \frac{\rho\theta_1}{2}\right) + 2\rho C(Z_B + Z_A)}{4Z_B - 4Z_A + 3\rho Z_A}.$$

Although these expression are considerably more complex than their counterparts in equation (5), the same general conclusions hold here as well. In particular, tedious calculation demonstrates that $P_B^* > P_A^*$, and that P_B^* is increasing in Z_B and decreasing in Z_A. More importantly from our perspective, the number of customers purchasing cellular service is increasing in Z_B and Z_A. In particular,

Proposition A.1   Aggregate sales are increasing in Z_B.

Proof: Using the envelope theorem, the change in quantity induced by a change in Z_B is

$$\frac{\partial q}{\partial Z_B} = \frac{\partial q_A}{\partial Z_B} + \frac{\partial q_B}{\partial Z_B} = \rho \frac{P_B - P_A}{(Z_B - Z_A)^2} + (1-\rho)\frac{P_A - \theta_2}{Z_B^2} - \rho \frac{P_B - P_A}{(Z_B - Z_A)^2} = \frac{P_A - \theta}{Z_B^2} > 0.$$

∎

Appendix B - Intensive Margin Model

In this appendix, we consider an alternative modification to equation 1. In contrast to the assumptions in the text, here we assume that all consumers purchase the good, but that q_j is not limited to 0 or 1. Specifically, let $q_j() = Z_j - P_j$ for $j = A, B$ where the decision regarding which firm to buy from is determined by the same inequality as in text (e.g., buy from B if $x_i Z_B - P_B > x_i Z_A - P_A$). We can then write firm B's demand as

$$q_B = \left(1 - \frac{P_B - P_A}{Z_B - Z_A}\right)(Z_B - P_B).$$

So that its objective function is

$$\Pi_B = \left(1 - \frac{P_B - P_A}{Z_B - Z_A}\right)(Z_B - P_B)(P_B - C).$$

and its first-order condition with respect to P_B is

$$0 = 3P_B^2 - 2P_B(2Z_B - Z_A + C + P_A) + CZ_B + (Z_B + C)(Z_B - Z_A + P_A).$$

It can be shown that the derivative of P_B with respect to Z_B is positive and the derivative with respect to Z_A is negative (i.e., B's best-response function is increasing in Z_B and decreasing in Z_A).

Because all customers are assumed to buy the good,

$$q_A = \int_0^{\frac{P_B - P_A}{Z_B - Z_A}} (Z_A - P_A) \, dx = \left(\frac{P_B - P_A}{Z_B - Z_A}\right)(Z_A - P_A)$$

so that A's objective function is

$$\Pi_A = \frac{P_B - P_A}{Z_B - Z_A}(Z_A - P_A)(P_A - C)$$

and its first-order condition with respect to P_A is

$$0 = 3P_A^2 - 2P_A(Z_A + C + P_B) + Z_A C + (Z_A + C)P_B.$$

Proposition A.2: Let P_i^* be the equilibrium value of firm i's price, then $\partial P_B^*/\partial Z_B > \partial P_A^*/\partial Z_B > 0$.
Proof: Using the implicit function theorem, we note that the derivative of P_A with respect to Z_B is zero, while an increase in Z_B shifts out B's best-response function. Therefore, as long as both best-response functions are upward sloping, and the slopes are less than one, an equilibrium exists whereby both prices are increasing in Z_B. The slope of A's best response function is

$$\frac{\partial P_A(P_B)}{\partial P_B} = \frac{2P_A - Z_A - C}{6P_A - 2P_B - 2(Z_A + C)}.$$

Rewriting the denominator as $2(2P_A - Z_A - C) + 2(P_A - P_B)$, it follows that the slope of A's best response function is between 0 and 1/2. Similar analysis shows that $\partial P_B/\partial P_A$ is between 0 and 1/2. Since $\partial P_A/\partial P_B$ < 1, it follows that $\partial P_B/\partial Z_B > \partial P_A/\partial Z_B$. ∎

Proposition A.3 Aggregate quantity sold is increasing in Z_B.

Proof: Using the envelope theorem, the change in quantity induced by a change in Z_B is

$$\frac{\partial q}{\partial Z_B} = \frac{\partial q_A}{\partial Z_B} + \frac{\partial q_B}{\partial Z_B} = \left(\frac{Z_B - Z_A + P_A - P_B}{Z_B - Z_A} \right) \left(1 + \frac{P_B - P_A}{Z_B - Z_A} \right).$$

which is positive iff $Z_B - Z_A > P_B - P_A$. To see that this condition holds, note that $\partial P_B/\partial Z_B$ (holding P_A constant) < 1/2. Since $\partial P_A/\partial Z_B = 0$ and $0 < \partial P_A/\partial P_B < 1$, it follows that the increase in P_B must be less than the increase in Z_B, and a fortiori that $P_B - P_A$ increases less than Z_B. Since when $Z_B = Z_A$, $P_B = P_A$, higher Z_B results in greater difference between Z_B and Z_A than between P_B and P_A. ∎

Unlike the other derivatives, the relationship between P_A and Z_A is not monotonic;

$$\frac{\partial P_A}{\partial Z_A} = \frac{2P_A - P_B - C}{6P_A - 2P_B - 2(Z_A + C)}.$$

In general, we cannot sign this derivative. This indeterminacy reflects the logic that reductions in Z_A have two offsetting effects. As Z_A falls, A's demand shifts in, but becomes less elastic. The elasticity effect reflects the principle that A's remaining customers do not value quality as much as its departing customers, and hence view B's higher price/higher quality product as a weaker substitute than do the departing customers.

Where the derivative is non-positive, the net effect of higher Z_A (less discrimination) is to reduce both prices. When it is positive, the net effect on both prices of higher Z_A is ambiguous. Importantly for our results, we do know that equilibrium prices are decreasing in Z_A for small amounts of discrimination. That is, in the neighborhood of $Z_A = Z_B$, P_A and P_B rise as Z_A falls, since we know that $P_A = P_B = C$ at $Z_A = Z_B$, while $P_A > C$ when Z_A is slightly less than Z_B. Conversely, in the neighborhood of $Z_A = C$, P_A falls with Z_A, since P_A approaches c as Z_A approaches c. In general, we would expect P_B to be monotonically decreasing in Z_A, while P_A would be increasing in Z_A when Z_A is small, and decreasing in

Z_A as Z_A approaches Z_B. Figure A1 presents a simulation of the effect of Z_A on prices. This simulation suggests that the predictions of the discrimination hypothesis for prices will not distinguish between the two hypotheses. That is, a finding that both prices are increasing in the degree of integration is consistent with both the discrimination and efficiency hypotheses. However, there is a difference between the hypotheses in regard to the effect of integration on output.

Proposition A.4: Greater discrimination leads to a reduction in aggregate sales.

Proof: Taking the derivative of $q_B + q_A$ with respect to Z_A, we get $\partial q / \partial Z_A = (P_B - P_A)^2 / (Z_B - Z_A) > 0$. Hence, greater discrimination reduces sales. ∎

Figure A1
The Effect of Discrimination on Prices (for C = 1, Z_B = 10)

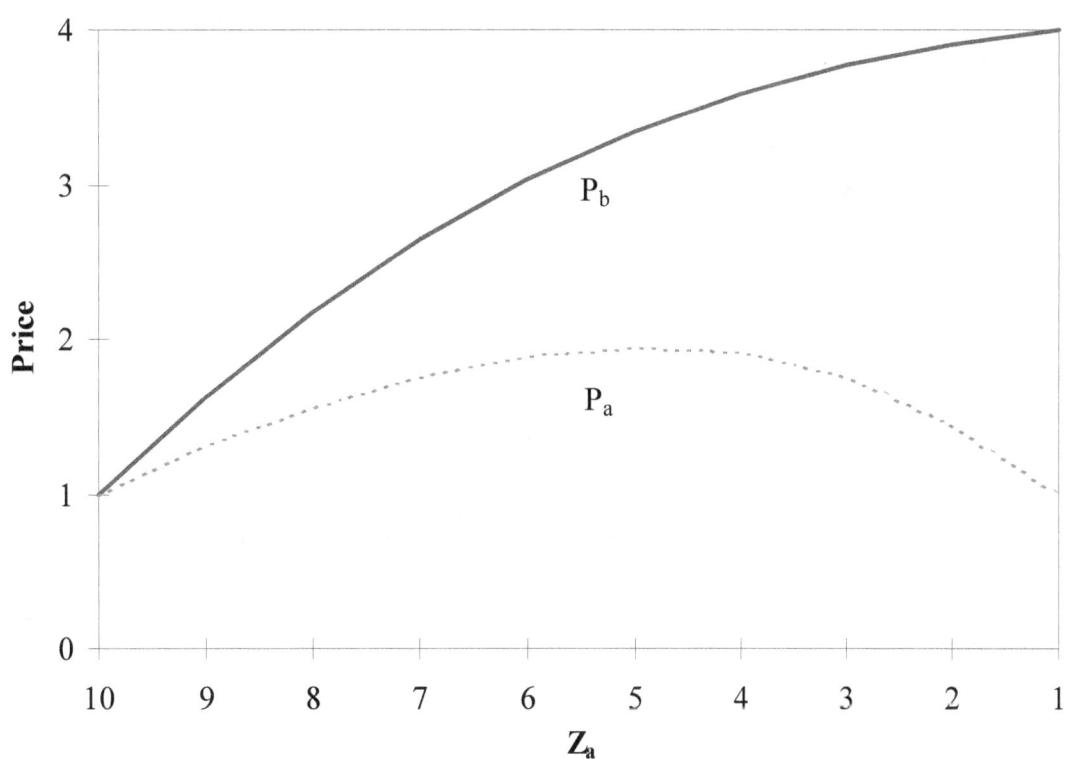